Homemad

from Head to Toes

Easy All-Natural Beauty Products Recipes for Skin, Hair and Nails

Josephine Simon

ISBN: 9781095700044

Printed in the United States

MAPLEWOOD
— PUBLISHING —

Contents

Introduction

"Beauty is in the mind of the beholder" goes a famous saying. However, that has never stopped people from trying various ways to enhance their physical appearance. After all, as Keats tells us, "A thing of beauty is a joy forever". The ever-expanding market for beauty products proves him right. Here is what is wrong: Beauty products, along with just about everything else, have strayed far from nature. This is precisely the point of this book, to help people look beautiful and radiant in the most natural way—yes, **from head to toe with 100% natural homemade products.**

This book covers beauty needs for both women and men.

You will learn:
- Reasons why you should go all-natural
- Skin types and how to care for them
- How to make natural beauty products at home—everything from scrubs to moisturizers to makeup remover—from head to toe
- How to treat acne, dark circles, hair loss and other cosmetic problems
- How to follow a healthy lifestyle
- And a lot more.

Why Use Homemade Beauty Products

When there's such a wide range of products available in supermarkets and drugstores, when online shopping gives you endless choices in the comfort of your own home (plus free delivery and returns in many cases)—is there any reason you should make beauty products at home? Well, there are more reasons than one!

1) You Are Safe
Sounds out of context? Well, beauty products sold in the supermarket can contain ingredients that may be very harmful to your skin—more harmful than you could ever imagine. Even those products that make the "all-natural" claim may not be produced with your interests in mind. Making your own beauty products keeps you healthy and safe.

2) You Know What Is in What You Use
This is one of the most important benefits of making natural beauty products at home. You know each and every ingredient you add to your beauty product. Though the label on store-bought products gives a list of the ingredients, it is never complete. There are always ingredients you never realize the product contains. But you're using these products on your skin, so it's best you know them inside out.

3) You Have Creative Space
Even if you are a very busy person, it is still fun to make beauty products for your own use. You can get creative by adding or excluding any ingredient in a given recipe. For example, if you prefer a specific essential oil over another that is used in a store-

bought product, you can try it when you make the product on your own. Things may not work all the time, but it will still be a fun learning experience.

4) You Can Save Money and Look More Radiant Too
Making your own beauty products will save you more money than you can imagine! Products that are expensive in the supermarket can be made for much less at home—and although the expensive products are made for specific skin types, they're not made specifically for *you*! When you make your own beauty product, you make it for yourself and no one else—and who knows better than you what works for your skin?

5) You Can Create Multi-Purpose Products
Most commercial beauty products offer super-specialized properties for one specific purpose; a skin toner is specifically designed to tone your skin and a moisturizer is only a moisturizer and so on. When you make your own beauty products, you know the ingredients you are adding, and you also know how they can work for more than one need. Now a skin toner can be a moisturizer, and an acne remover can also be a deodorant and an aftershave. When you can create one product with multiple uses, you spend less and gain more.

6) Your Gifts Can Get Creative and Cost-Effective
Who wouldn't love to be given homemade natural beauty products? By giving your beauty products as gifts, you not only make the recipients happy—you also save money for yourself.

7) You Can Run Your Own Business
Your handmade beauty products not only make you glow—they can also make you a successful businessperson. The growing demand for beauty products, particularly homemade, will make it easy to start a successful business.

8) You Are Environment-Friendly

From the chemicals and preservatives involved in making the beauty products sold in the supermarket, to the plastic involved in the packaging, the damage caused to the environment is unimaginable. When making beauty products at home, you use only 100% natural ingredients, thereby doing your part to save the Earth.

9) You Are Empowered

You are able to create your own beauty products; you look stunning using your own natural products; you help create awareness of the benefits of using homemade natural products; you run a successful business that really serves people and the Earth—How empowered do you feel about all these? You feel *absolutely* empowered, right? And when you feel empowered, you have a higher confidence level, increased productivity, and ongoing success.

Life, after all, is all about how you feel about yourself and how you contribute to society. Making your own natural products without compromising your ethics can be a great experience. Are you ready for it?

Skin Types and Associated Issues

Not all skin types are created equal. Not all skin conditions affect different skin types the same. Knowing your skin type helps you decide on what is right for your skin and how to achieve and maintain healthy skin.

Types of Skin

Skin can be broadly classified into four types. They are:

Normal Skin

Normal skin is neither dry nor oily. It is well-balanced healthy skin. With good blood circulation, normal skin looks radiant. The pores are very small and the skin has hardly any blemishes. Generally, young people have normal skin.

Associated Problems
- Suntan after exposure to strong sun
- Dry skin during winter

These problems are easily addressed, so it's a real blessing to have normal skin.

Oily Skin

Oily skin looks thick, plump and shiny, with visible pores. This type of skin is susceptible to conditions such as acne. Apart from genetics, factors such as stress and hormonal changes can cause oily skin. Oily skin is common in men and during adolescence.

Associated Problems
- Sweaty look
- Pimples
- Acne
- Large pores
- No improvement with repeated washing

Dry Skin

Dry skin lacks elasticity and the pores are hardly visible. Wrinkles appear sooner in dry skin. This type of skin causes the complexion to look dull and rough. Dry skin is prone to infection, itching and cracking. It is more common in women.

Associated Problems
- Occurrence of wrinkles and fine lines in younger people
- Itching
- Prone to skin infections
- Eczema
- Rashes

Combination Skin

Combination skin is a mix of dry skin and oily skin. Those with combination skin often have oily skin on their forehead, nose and chin and dry skin around their eyes, cheeks and mouth. Combination skin is susceptible to large pores and acne in areas of oily skin.

Associated Problems

- Forehead, nose and chin—called the T-zone—get very shiny
- Occurrence of pimples and blackheads in T-zone
- Wrinkles and skin inflammation in cheeks

Getting Your Toolbox Ready

Your toolbox says it all. The better equipped you are, the more productive you'll be and the better the outcome is. Not having a particular tool when you are otherwise all set to make a new beauty product can be very discouraging, so the rule is to start from the start—that is, to get your toolbox ready first.

Tools Required

Your kitchen cabinet often takes on the role of medicine cabinet as it stores ingredients that serve as home remedies to treat various health conditions. It's also something of a toolbox, as it already contains many of the tools you'll need to create your own beauty products at home. So you can start gathering your tools from here—although, of course, you can always go out to buy new ones if you don't want to use your kitchen utensils for this purpose. Here's a list of what to assemble:

- Wooden, bamboo, metal and plastic spoons
- Spatula
- Hand blender
- Measuring beakers or cups
- Mixing bowls
- Saucepans
- Knives
- Chopping board
- Sieve
- Spray bottles
- Pipette

- Toothpicks
- Storage containers
- Double boiler maker
- Double boiler insert
- Mortar and pestle
- Coffee grinder
- Rubber gloves
- Mesh strainer
- Kitchen scale
- Weighing dishes
- Funnel
- Thermometer
- pH strips
- Molds

Finally, remember to buy dish detergent so you can keep your tools clean after use.

Main Ingredients Used, Their Properties and Benefits

Having a toolbox ready to make your own beauty products is the first step. The next to follow naturally is to have ready stock of the main ingredients that are used to make all-natural beauty products in the comfort of your home. Here is a list of main ingredients to get you started. Their properties and benefits are additionally provided so you will know why you are using a particular ingredient for a particular purpose and it also helps you to get creative and use a particular ingredient given for a particular recipe for other recipes based on your needs.

Ingredients	Properties	Benefits
Almond oil	Anti-inflammatory, emollient, a rich source of vitamin E	Treats skin conditions Softens the skin Improves skin health Postpones aging symptoms
Aloe vera	Antioxidant, antibacterial, Antiviral, antimicrobial, anti-inflammatory, antiseptic	Heals skin problems Softens the skin Promotes skin glow
Amla	Anti-inflammatory, antioxidant, antibacterial	Aids in detoxification Cleanses the blood and promotes skin glow Postpones signs of aging

Apple cider vinegar	Antibacterial, antifungal	Prevents hair damage, promotes hair glow
Baking soda	Anti-inflammatory, antiseptic	Heals acne breakouts, exfoliates the skin
Bentonite clay	Moisturizer, detoxifying	Heals skin conditions, aids in skin detoxification
Banana	Anti-inflammatory, antioxidant, antidepressant, moisturizer	Moisturizes the skin, lightens dark spots in skin, postpones aging symptoms
Beeswax	Antibacterial, antimicrobial, anti-inflammatory, astringent	Heals skin conditions, lightens skin tone, moisturizes the skin, heals cracked lips
Beetroot	Anti-inflammatory, antioxidant	Lightens dark lips, works as a natural dye
Bergamot essential oil	Antibiotic, deodorant, antiseptic	Works as deodorant
Black tea	Antioxidant, antibacterial, anti-inflammatory	Boosts immune function, prevents tooth decay
Brown sugar	Anti-inflammatory, antimicrobial	Protects skin health
Butter	Antioxidant, antibacterial, antifungal	Hydrates the skin, softens lips
Calendula oil	Antibacterial, antifungal, anti-inflammatory	Heals skin conditions, soothes skin
Candelilla wax	Anti-inflammatory	Soothes the skin, heals skin conditions, hydrates the skin

Carrot seed	Antioxidant, antiseptic, stimulant, detoxifier	Protects skin, postpones signs of aging
Castor oil	Moisturizer, antibacterial, anti-inflammatory, emollient	Soothes skin, treats wrinkles, promotes hair growth
Chamomile herb	Antibacterial, anti-inflammatory	Soothes skin, heals skin problems
Charcoal	Anti-inflammatory, antibacterial	Heals acne, promotes skin health
Cinnamon	Anti-inflammatory, antioxidant, antifungal	Heals acne, improves skin tone, prevents aging symptoms, supports hair health
Clove	Anti-inflammatory, antiviral, antioxidant, antifungal	Cures acne, relieves tooth pain, cures sores
Cocoa butter	Anti-inflammatory, antioxidant	Postpones aging symptoms, supports hair health, improves skin health
Coconut oil	Anti-inflammatory, antimicrobial, moisturizer, antibacterial	Moisturizes the skin, fights tooth decay, supports hair growth, softens the lips
Coffee grounds	Antibacterial, antimicrobial	Treats acne, improves tone of lips, heals dark circles
Cucumber	Antibacterial, antimicrobial, antioxidant, antifungal	Hydrates lips, hydrates skin, cures pigmentation, heals puffy eyes, treats wrinkles

Curd	Antibacterial, antimicrobial	Supports hair growth and makes the hair glow, moisturizes the skin, reduces fine lines
Curry leaves	Antibacterial, antioxidant, antimicrobial	Promotes hair growth, postpones graying of hair
Egg white	Antibacterial, antimicrobial	Tightens the skin, improves skin tone, promotes hair growth
Epsom salt	Antimicrobial, antibacterial	Relaxes muscles, moisturizes the lips
Eucalyptus essential oil	Antibacterial, antiseptic, antimicrobial	Soothes the skin, hydrates the skin, improves hair growth
Frankincense essential oil	Anti-inflammatory, antiseptic, antimicrobial	Treats acne, tightens the skin, prevents wrinkles
Garlic	Antibacterial, antimicrobial, antiviral	Heals cold sores, treats nail fungus, fights acne
Geranium	Antibacterial, antimicrobial, anti-inflammatory, antiseptic	Boosts skin health, cures acne
Ginger	Antibacterial, antiseptic, antimicrobial	Treats wrinkles, tones the skin, cures acne
Glycerin	Antibacterial, antifungal	Tones and hydrates the skin, treats wrinkles
Gram flour	Antibacterial, antimicrobial	Tightens the skin, prevents wrinkles

Grapefruit essential oil	Antioxidant, antiseptic, antibacterial, antimicrobial	Heals acne, promotes hair growth
Green tea	Antioxidant, antibacterial, antimicrobial	Tones the skin, promotes skin health, treats puffy eyes, exfoliates the skin
Hazelnut oil	Antibacterial, antioxidant, astringent	Cleanses and moisturizes the skin, supports nail health
Honey	Antibacterial, antimicrobial, antioxidant, moisturizer	Moisturizes and hydrates the skin, lightens lip tone, improves skin tone, treats wrinkles, cures acne
Hydrogen peroxide	Antimicrobial, antibacterial	Heals acne, removes stains on teeth
Jojoba oil	Anti-inflammatory, antimicrobial, antibacterial, moisturizer	Tones the skin, heals skin conditions, reduces skin inflammation
Lavender essential oil	Anti-inflammatory, antiseptic, antimicrobial, antibacterial, antifungal	Supports skin health, reduces fine lines, lightens skin tone
Lemon balm	Antioxidant, antibacterial, antimicrobial	Heals cold sores
Lemon essential oil	Anti-inflammatory, antibacterial, antioxidant	Brightens skin tone, heals skin conditions
Lemon juice	Antibacterial, antimicrobial	Cures acne, moisturizes the skin, prevents wrinkles, lightens dark lips, supports hair growth

Liquid castile soap	Antibacterial	Cleanses the skin, treats acne, helps to maintain pH balance of the skin
Milk	Antibacterial, antimicrobial	Softens the skin, moisturizes and improves skin tone, heals acne, treats puffy eyes, reduces pigmentation
Mint leaves	Antioxidant, antibacterial	Cures puffy eyes and dark circles under the eyes, improves skin tone, hydrates the skin, cures acne
Myrrh	Antibacterial, antimicrobial, antioxidant	Supports skin health, reduces fine lines, heals sores
Neem leaves	Antibacterial, antifungal, antiviral, antimicrobial	Cures acne, promotes skin glow, heals skin conditions, postpones signs of aging
Non-nano zinc oxide	Antibacterial	Protects skin from UV rays, prevents burns
Oats	Antioxidant, antibacterial, antimicrobial	Cures pigmentation, exfoliates the skin, promotes skin health, cures sunburn
Olive oil	Antibacterial, antifungal, anti-inflammatory, antimicrobial	Moisturizes the skin, prevents wrinkles, hydrates the lips, promotes skin health, exfoliates the skin
Onion juice	Antibacterial, antimicrobial, anti-inflammatory	Promotes hair growth, cures pigmentation, supports skin health

Orange juice	Anti-inflammatory	Cures acne, postpones signs of aging, tones and brightens the skin
Oregano essential oil	Anti-inflammatory, antibacterial, antimicrobial	Cures nail fungus, cures acne, promotes hair growth, cures dandruff
Peppermint essential oil	Antibacterial, antifungal, antiseptic, anti-microbial,	Cleanses the skin, improves oral health, cures acne, promotes hair growth
Pineapple	Anti-inflammatory, Antibacterial	Treats wrinkles, cures acne, improves skin tone, promotes hair growth
Potato	Antioxidant, Anti-inflammatory	Treats puffy eyes, improves skin tone, promotes hair growth, treats wrinkles, heals dark circles under eyes
Potato peels	Anti-inflammatory, antioxidant	Lighten hair color, treats acne, improves skin health, promotes skin tone
Red raspberry seed oil	Anti-inflammatory, antioxidant	Protects skin from UV rays, treats acne, firms the skin, prevents premature aging
Rose water	Anti-inflammatory, antimicrobial	Cleanses and moisturizes the skin, treats acne, promotes skin health
Rosemary essential oil	Anti-inflammatory, antioxidant	Treats acne, promotes skin glow, supports hair growth
Rosemary herb	Anti-inflammatory, antioxidant	Protects skin health, supports hair health

Sage leaves	Antifungal, antimicrobial, anti-inflammatory	Treats wrinkles, improves skin conditions, prevents graying of hair, promotes hair growth
Sandalwood essential oil	Anti-inflammatory, antiseptic, antibacterial, astringent	Heals skin conditions, promotes skin glow, postpones signs of aging, moisturizes the skin, promotes hair growth
Sea salt	Antibacterial, antimicrobial	Exfoliates the skin, prevents acne, moisturizes the skin, fights dandruff, promotes dental hygiene
Shea butter	Antioxidant, moisturizer, anti-microbial, Anti-inflammatory	Moisturizes the skin, heals acne, treats fine lines and wrinkles, reduces stretch marks
Sugar	Antibacterial, antimicrobial	Exfoliates the skin, promotes skin glow
Tea tree oil	Antiviral, antibacterial, anti-inflammatory, antifungal	Improves skin health, cures acne, heals nail fungus, hydrates the skin
Thyme	Antifungal, antibacterial, antibacterial	Heals acne, promotes skin health and glow, prevents premature aging symptoms, protects skin from UV rays, promotes hair growth
Tomato	Antioxidant, antimicrobial, anti-inflammatory	Prevents wrinkles, protects skin from UV rays, aids in skin regeneration, promotes skin tone

Trace minerals	Antibacterial	Promotes skin health, maintain skin elasticity, prevents wrinkles
Turmeric	Antibacterial, antimicrobial, anti-inflammatory	Heals acne, promotes skin regeneration, maintains a youthful appearance, treats stretch marks, reduces dark circles under eyes
Vanilla	Antioxidant, antimicrobial	Cures cold sores, treats acne, soothes the skin, promotes skin health, supports hair health
Vaseline	Antibacterial, antimicrobial	Treats dry lips, moisturizes the skin
Vitamin E oil	Antioxidant, antimicrobial, antibacterial, anti-fungal	Reduces marks on the skin, soothes and moisturizes the skin, minimizes wrinkles, promotes hair growth
Wheat germ oil	Antioxidant, antibacterial	Prevents symptoms of aging, improves skin tone, supports skin health, nourishes the hair
Yogurt	Anti-inflammatory, antimicrobial	Heals acne, prevents sagging of skin, treats wrinkles, moisturizes the skin, minimizes dark circles under eyes

Face Care Complete Guide for Radiance

It is quite natural that we start with the face. This chapter is a complete guide to maintaining a healthy glow in your face, from how to wash your face to how to postpone signs of facial aging.

How to Wash Your Face the Right Way

It turns out there are more than a couple of *wrong* ways to wash your face. It's not just splashing some water, scrubbing with a cleanser and splashing some more water to remove the cleanser. There are a few finer aspects you should remember when you wash your face:

- Wash your face with cool or lukewarm water. Do not use hot water, as it causes dry skin.
- Apply a gentle cleanser using your fingertips. Scrubs are too hard for your facial skin and using them may result in over-exfoliation, which does more harm than good to your face.
- Do not scrub your face. Your facial skin is very soft, and scrubbing it could cause skin irritation and even wrinkles.
- Rinse your face with lukewarm water.
- Pat dry using a soft towel.
- If you have dry skin, apply a moisturizer after washing.

- Wash your face twice a day—once in the morning and once before going to bed. If you have sweated excessively, you can wash your face in between, but never over-wash your face.
- Using toner after washing your face helps rebalance your skin. Follow up the toner with moisturizer or serum to keep your skin hydrated.

Do It Yourself!
Every Beauty Product You Will Ever Want

This will get you started—and then some! This chapter covers the making of:

- Facial creams
- Lotions
- Moisturizers
- Toners
- Sunscreens
- Face scrubs
- Face washes
- Face masks
- Makeup removers
- Facial steams

The Difference between Cream, Lotion, Moisturizer, and Toner

If you wonder about the difference between cream and lotion and toner and moisturizer, you are not alone. Many go for cream when they actually need a lotion—and vice versa. Knowing each of these products will help you make an informed decision while choosing ingredients to customize your beauty products.

Cream

A combination of oil and water, cream is high in oil content, greasy and with a thick consistency. It nourishes and hydrates the skin. Cream is especially great for dry to very dry skin and during harsh, arid weather.

Lotion

Lotion is a blend of water and oil where the water content is much higher than the oil content. It is non-greasy and light. It works great for hydrating skin that is not too dry. Lotion is best used during summer or in humid climates.

Moisturizer

Moisturizer is a must-have for all skin types. Moisturizer contains water and oils or humectants and checks moisture loss. It absorbs water and retains moisture in the skin. Moisturizer prevents skin irritation and soothes the skin.

Toner

Toner removes leftover makeup, dirt and traces of oil, cleans the skin and shrinks pores. It restores the pH balance of the skin. Toner is applied after face wash and before moisturizer. Toner is highly effective in treating various skin conditions, including acne.

Facial Cream

There are quite a number of ways in which you can make facial creams at home with minimal, easily available ingredients.

Facial Cream No. 1

Ingredients
½ cup almond oil
¼ cup coconut oil
2 tablespoons shea butter
¼ cup beeswax
Few drops of tea tree oil (you can also add any other essential oil that benefits your skin)

Preparation
1. Simmer some water in a pot. Add everything except the tea tree oil to a jar and place the jar in the water. Stir occasionally until the ingredients in the jar melt. Remove the jar from the water. Add a few drops of essential oil and mix well. Close the jar and leave it to cool and harden at room temperature.

Facial Cream No. 2—Using Essential Oils

Ingredients

3 tablespoons melted beeswax

¾ cup coconut oil or almond oil (or any carrier oil you prefer)

5 drops each of essential oil of

- Lavender
- Geranium
- Frankincense
- Carrot Seed
- Myrrh
- Tea Tree

Preparation

1. Add about 2 inches of water to a baking pan and place the pan over low heat. Add beeswax pearls to a mixing bowl and place the bowl in the water. Stir occasionally until the beeswax melts. Pour the coconut oil into a bowl and whip it with a hand mixer until it gets fluffy. Add the essential oils to the whipped coconut oil and mix well. Now add the melted beeswax and whip until everything is well blended.

Lotion

Every step you take in making your own beauty product, you are progressing—even when you seem to be taking two steps back! Experience makes you wiser, and before you realize it you'll have a whole lot of success stories to share. The recipes given here are just starters to get you going.

Lotion No. 1

Ingredients
½ cup coconut oil or olive oil or jojoba oil
¼ cup shea butter
5 drops essential oil (lavender or tea tree or carrot seed)

Preparation
1. Fill a pot about a quarter full with water and place it on the stove over low heat. Add the shea butter to a heat-safe glass bowl (like Pyrex) and place the bowl in the pot on the stove. Melt the shea butter, then add the coconut oil and turn off the heat. You can also whip the shea butter instead of melting it, then add the coconut oil to it and mix well. If you melt the shea butter, you'll need to refrigerate it until it becomes slightly firm. After it does, add the essential oil. Whip it well so the ingredients blend. Store it in a jar at room temperature.

Lotion No. 2

For making herbal oil
Dried chamomile
Dried rosemary
Coconut oil

For making lotion with herbal oil
1 cup herbal oil
½ cup distilled water
¼ cup beeswax

Making Herbal Oil
1. Chop the herbs finely and add them to a glass jar. Add coconut oil to the jar until the herbs are soaked. Close with a tight-fitting lid. Place the jar in a cool, dark place. After a week, strain the oil through a strainer. Press the herbs in the strainer with the back of a spoon to extract as much oil as possible. Store the oil in a glass jar.

Making Lotion
1. Fill a pot one-third full with water and place it on the stove over low heat. Add the herbal oil and beeswax to a bowl and place it in the pot. Turn off the heat after the beeswax melts. Blend the mixture well, adding the distilled water little by little as you blend until the desired consistency is reached. Store in a glass jar.

Moisturizers

Making moisturizers at home can get very interesting, particularly when you test the results. But don't worry—even if you don't get the combination right initially, you have the space to make a product that is truly yours, and you'll probably succeed on your next attempt.

Moisturizer No. 1

Ingredients
1 cup olive oil
1 cup coconut oil or almond oil
½ cup beeswax or candelilla wax

Preparation
1. Place a pan on the stove, fill it about one-third full with water, and heat it over low heat. Add the olive oil, coconut oil and beeswax to a bowl and place the bowl in the pan. After the beeswax melts, turn off the heat and remove the bowl from the pan. Allow the moisturizer to cool. Whisk it well until it thickens.

Moisturizer No. 2

Ingredients

1 tablespoon honey

1 tablespoon almond oil or coconut oil

2 teaspoons rose water or lemon juice

2 tablespoons cocoa butter

Preparation

1. Add the almond oil and cocoa butter to a bowl. Place it in a pan filled one-third full with water. Heat the pan until the cocoa butter melts. Remove from heat. Add the honey and rose water and let it cool.

Toner

Toner does more than remove your makeup. It maintains the pH balance of your skin, which is great for acne prone skin. Making your own toner can be a great way to treat your skin.

Toner No. 1

Ingredients
1 tablespoon honey
1 teaspoon fresh lemon juice
½ apple, cut into pieces

Preparation
1. Whisk the honey and lemon juice together in a bowl. Blend the apple pieces in a blender. Add the blended apple to the honey and lemon juice and mix well.

Toner No. 2

Ingredients
Juice from ½ lemon, or lemon peels

1. Yes, it's as simple as that! All you need to do is massage your face with lemon peels or lemon juice.

Toner No. 3

Ingredients

1 teaspoon green tea

¼ cup cucumber juice

Preparation

1. Add the green tea to ½ cup of boiled water and let it steep for about 5 minutes. Strain the leaves and let the tea cool. Extract the cucumber juice and filter it. Mix the juice and tea together and blend well.

Sunscreens

Sunscreen prevents symptoms of premature aging. It protects the skin from the ill effects of ultraviolet rays and promotes skin health.

Sunscreen No. 1

Ingredients
1 cup coconut oil
¼ cup non-nano zinc oxide
2 tablespoons red raspberry seed oil
Few drops of carrot seed essential oil

Preparation
1. Blend the coconut oil in a mixing bowl. Add all other ingredients to the coconut oil and mix thoroughly.

Sunscreen No. 2

Ingredients
4 drops peppermint oil
4 drops lavender oil
1 cup rose water

Preparation
1. Mix all ingredients and blend until frothy.

Face Scrub

A face scrub removes dead skin cells, oil and dirt that tend to accumulate on the skin surface. Applying makeup after exfoliating your skin with a face scrub leaves your skin glowing. Use a face scrub once or twice a week.

Face Scrub No. 1

Ingredients

1 tablespoon green tea
1 tablespoon honey
1 tablespoon sugar

Preparation

1. Add the green tea to 1 cup of boiling water. Let it cool and then strain out the leaves. Add the honey and sugar to the green tea and mix well until the ingredients blend.

Face Scrub No. 2

Ingredients

3 tablespoons honey
1 tablespoon cinnamon powder, freshly ground

Preparation

1. Mix the honey and cinnamon powder thoroughly to make a smooth paste.

Face Wash

Unless you're fine with using only water to wash your face, you will need a face wash to keep your skin clean and glowing.

Face Wash No. 1

Ingredients
1 teaspoon fresh lemon juice
2 teaspoons honey

Preparation
1. Mix the lemon juice and honey in a mixing bowl until the ingredients blend.
2. Apply the face wash to your face and neck and let it dry. Rinse off with warm water after 20 minutes.

Face Wash No. 2

Ingredients
1 teaspoon honey
2 teaspoons raw milk

Preparation
1. Thoroughly mix the honey and raw milk in a mixing bowl until the ingredients blend well.
2. Apply the face wash to your face and gently massage for about 3 minutes. Rinse with warm water after a few minutes.

Face Mask

A face mask keeps your skin hydrated. It promotes better skin tone, reduces fine lines, makes the skin firm, and helps to maintain youthful appearance.

Face Mask No. 1

Ingredients

1 ripe banana
Few drops of honey

Preparation

1. Mash the banana. Add the honey and blend to make a smooth paste. Apply the face mask to your face and neck. Leave it for 15 to 20 minutes, then rinse well with cold water.

Face Mask No. 2

Ingredients

1 tablespoon milk
1 tablespoon honey

Preparation

1. Thoroughly mix the milk and honey in a mixing bowl. Apply the face mask to your face and neck. Leave it for 15 to 10 minutes, then rinse off with cold water.

Makeup Remover

Removing your makeup at the end of the day is just as important as wearing your makeup correctly!

Makeup Remover No. 1

Ingredients
¾ cup coconut oil or olive oil
¼ cup hazelnut oil

Preparation
1. Blend the oils. Apply the makeup remover to your face and massage gently for a few minutes. Dip a clean cotton cloth in hot water, wring it and place the cloth over your face. Let it stay there for a minute and then wipe your face with a clean cloth.

Makeup Remover No. 2

Ingredients
Aloe vera juice extracted from one fresh leaf
3 to 4 drops of olive oil or coconut oil

Preparation
1. Blend even parts of aloe vera juice and olive oil thoroughly. Apply the makeup remover to your face. Wipe it off after few minutes.

Facial Steams

Before we proceed into the making of facial steams at home, let's learn why it is important to steam your face.

Benefits of Facial Steaming

- Unclogs the pores by releasing dead skin cells
- Boosts blood circulation
- Boosts production of collagen, which makes the skin glow, improves elasticity and promotes a youthful appearance
- Hydrates the skin and treats dry skin
- Clears the skin of blackheads and whiteheads
- Checks acne outbursts
- Relieves sinus congestion
- Postpones symptoms of aging
- Relaxes the body and mind

Facial Steam

Ingredients
Pot of hot water
Few drops of essential oil (optional; choose based on your skin type or need)
Dried herbs (optional)

Preparation
1. Wash your face with a mild cleanser to remove makeup and dirt. Boil some water in a pot. After the water boils, add the essential oil and remove from the stove. Transfer the essential oil infused water to a bowl and place it on a

flat surface. Drape a thick towel over your face and shoulders and bend over the bowl, maintaining a safe distance. Ensure the towel is draped well so no steam gets out. Steam your face for about 10 minutes. Splash some cold water on your face to close your pores. Apply moisturizer to your damp skin.

Facial steams should not be done more than once a week. Avoid them when you have acne breakouts or are experiencing inflammation of your facial skin.

The best herbs for various skin types include:

Normal Skin—Lavender, chamomile, lemon balm, peppermint
Oily Skin—Lavender, basil, chamomile
Dry Skin—Lavender, chamomile, comfrey, rose
Combination Skin—Rosemary, calendula, chamomile
Acne-Prone Skin—Basil, white willow bark

Natural Treatment for Acne at Home

Acne outbreaks can have a devastating impact on your appearance. The causes for acne breakouts include family history, hormonal changes, lifestyle and stress. Given below are natural remedies to treat acne at home. They will help with outbreaks, but it's vital to address the root cause if you want to remain acne-free permanently.

1) Turmeric
Turmeric contains curcumin, which is anti-inflammatory. Its antioxidant, antibacterial and anti-fungal properties aid in curing acne.

Add one tablespoon of water to ¼ teaspoon of turmeric powder. Blend well to make a paste. Apply it to the affected area. Wash off after 10 to 15 minutes.

2) Honey
Honey possesses antibacterial properties which aid in treating acne. Honey keeps the skin hydrated. The glucose oxidase in honey helps to generate hydrogen peroxide, which checks breakouts of acne and fights bacterial infection.

Apply honey on the affected area. Wash off with water after 20 minutes.

3) Neem Leaves
Neem is anti-inflammatory and antibacterial and helps to treat skin conditions.

Grind a bunch of neem leaves to a fine paste by adding a few drops of water. Apply the paste to the affected area. Wash off with water after it dries.

4) Lemon Juice

Lemon juice contains citric acid, which is an antiseptic and hence supports treatment of acne.

Dip a cotton ball in fresh lemon juice and apply it to the affected area. Leave it to air dry before washing it off.

5) Sandalwood and Turmeric

The antimicrobial properties of sandalwood help to clear acne-causing bacteria. Turmeric is also antibacterial and anti-fungal.

Add one teaspoon each of sandalwood powder and turmeric powder to a mixing bowl. Add some water to make a fine paste. Apply it to the affected area. Wash off after it dries.

6) Aloe Vera

Aloe vera is antibacterial and is also effective in relieving inflammation caused by acne. It supports skin healing.

Carefully extract the gel from an aloe vera leaf. Apply it to the affected area. Leave it to be absorbed by the skin.

7) Clove and Honey

Clove and honey possess antibacterial properties. Clove is antiseptic, anti-fungal and antiviral and speeds up healing.

Add ½ teaspoon of honey to one teaspoon of clove powder and make a paste. Apply it to the affected area. Rinse after 15 minutes.

Natural Treatment for Wrinkles

Wrinkles, in the past, were telltale signs of aging. However, even young people get wrinkles these days! Stress—among various other factors—plays a vital role in wrinkle formation, and seeing wrinkles on your face will only add to your stress! Here are some of the best DIY remedies to treat those wrinkles.

1) Honey
Honey tightens the skin, thereby reducing wrinkles. Being a moisturizer, it promotes skin health and youthfulness as well.

Take a few drops of honey and apply it to your face. Massage gently for one or two minutes. Rinse after half an hour.

2) Ginger and Honey
If you have any apprehensions about using ginger, just try it once and you'll be a believer. Ginger checks the breakdown of elastin, which is a wrinkle-causing factor. Add a few drops of honey to one teaspoon of ginger extract. Blend well and apply to your wrinkles. Massage gently for a couple of minutes. Rinse after 15 minutes.

3) Tomato Juice
Being a rich source of vitamin C, tomato juice tightens skin and minimizes wrinkles. Tomato contains lycopene, which neutralizes the harmful effects of UV rays and checks free radicals which promote aging.

Apply juice from a ripe tomato to your face. Rinse after half an hour.

4) Cucumber

Cucumber hydrates the skin and promotes a youthful appearance.

Cucumber is effective for wrinkles around the eyes. Place cucumber slices on your closed eyes. Remove after 10 to 15 minutes. You can also rub cucumber on your face, as it prevents skin dryness.

5) Coconut Oil

The breakdown of collagen can cause wrinkles. Coconut oil promotes collagen production, thereby supporting the youthful appearance of skin. It is also a rich source of nutrients that prevent wrinkles.

Apply a few drops of coconut oil on your face and around your eyes. Massage for a few minutes. Allow it to be absorbed by your skin.

6) Olive Oil

Olive oil protects skin from dryness and prevents wrinkles. Oleic acid and polyphenols in olive oil help to retain moisture.

Apply 2 to 3 drops of olive oil to your face and under the eyes. You can also apply the oil at night and leave it overnight.

7) Castor Oil

Castor oil is very effective for wrinkles because it is an emollient, meaning that it has soothing properties. It is a wonderful moisturizer as well.

Apply one or two drops of castor oil to your face before bedtime. Allow it to be absorbed. Wash your face in the morning.

8) Milk, Honey and Turmeric

Milk and honey keep the skin moisturized. The curcumin in turmeric possesses antioxidant properties and helps destroy free radicals, thereby promoting a youthful appearance.

Add ½ teaspoon of turmeric to one teaspoon each of milk and honey and make a thick paste. Apply it to your face. Wash off after half an hour.

9) Green Tea

The antioxidant properties of green tea and the polyphenolic compounds it contains support skin health.

Dip a green tea bag or a teaspoon of green tea leaves in a glass of water. Remove the bag or filter out the leaves after a few minutes. Add honey and drink the tea twice or thrice a day.

You can place the dipped tea bags on your wrinkles for a few minutes and rinse off with water.

10) Banana, Honey and Lemon Juice

Banana removes dead skin cells and acts as a natural moisturizer, thereby maintaining skin health.

Mash a ripe banana. Add a few drops of honey and lemon juice to make a fine paste. Apply it to your face. Wash off after 20 minutes. You can also rub banana peel on your skin and rinse after 15 to 20 minutes.

Natural Anti-Aging Treatments

Here is an easy-to-make, all-natural anti-aging cream.

Anti-Aging Cream No. 1

Ingredients

1 teaspoon honey

2 teaspoons beeswax

1 tablespoon rose water

1 tablespoon shea butter

2 teaspoons wheat germ oil

Few drops almond oil

Preparation

1. Add water to a pan and place it on the stove. Add beeswax to a bowl and place it in the pan. Remove the bowl from the pan after the beeswax melts. Add the shea butter and mix thoroughly. Add the remaining ingredients and blend well. Store in an airtight container.

You can also use a banana mask, orange mask or honey mask to maintain youthfulness.

Natural Facelift Techniques

Facelift surgery is dangerous and expensive. Here are some of the best DIY facelift techniques which you can apply from the comfort of your home.

1) Honey and Gram Flour
Honey retains moisture and hydrates your skin, thereby keeping the skin youthful. Gram flour tightens the skin and prevents sagging of facial skin.

Add a few drops of honey to 2 to 3 teaspoons of gram flour. Add enough water to make a thick paste. Apply it to your face and neck. Use a damp cloth to wipe off after 15 minutes.

2) Egg White, Honey and Lemon Juice
Egg white contains albumin, which firms the skin and prevents sagging. Lemon moisturizes the skin, prevents wrinkles and tightens pores, thereby supporting a youthful appearance of the skin.

Add ½ teaspoon each of honey and lemon juice to 1 egg white and whip well. Apply to your face and rinse off after half an hour.

3) Banana
Banana hydrates the skin, promotes skin elasticity, and tightens the skin.

Mash a ripe banana. Add 2 tablespoons of honey and blend well. Apply the paste to your face. Rinse off after half an hour.

4) Yogurt
Yogurt contains lactic acid, which keeps the skin moisturized. The zinc in yogurt tightens skin tissues and prevents sagging.

Add a teaspoon of lemon juice to a teaspoon of yogurt and mix well. Apply to your face and massage for a couple of minutes. Wash off after 15 minutes.

How to Remove Facial Hair

Facial hair is a cause of concern for women, as it can negatively impact one's appearance. Here are some DIY home remedies to remove facial hair.

1) Turmeric

Turmeric contains curcumin, which reduces and prevents hair growth.

Combine two teaspoons of turmeric powder with enough water to make a paste. Apply the paste to the area of hair growth and let it dry. Clean with a cotton ball soaked in warm water.

2) Honey Wax

The combination of honey and lemon works great for removing facial hair because honey wax sticks to the skin and lemon exfoliates dead cells on the skin surface.

Add 1 cup of sugar to ¼ cup of honey. Mix in the juice of a medium-sized lemon. Blend thoroughly to make a paste. Apply it to the specific area, place a soft cotton cloth over it, and pull the cloth in the direction opposite the hair growth. This technique removes hair instantly. You can do it once a month or when necessity demands.

3) Egg

Egg sticks to the face, and when made into a paste with other necessary ingredients it helps to remove facial hair.

Add one tablespoon of sugar and ½ tablespoon of corn flour to the white of one egg. Blend well to make a paste. Apply it to the area where hair needs to be removed. Peel off gently after it dries.

Day and Night Care Tips to Make Your Face Glow

Following these day and night care techniques will give your face a healthy glow. Here is what you need to do:

- Wear sunscreen every day. Go for a sunscreen with SPF 30 or above.
- Remove your makeup before going to bed.
- Keep yourself hydrated. Drink enough water to see you through the day comfortably.
- Exfoliate your skin once or twice a week.
- Cleanse your face in the morning.
- Moisturize your face in the morning and before bedtime.

"The face is the index of the mind." Of course, this doesn't refer to external beauty, but you do get a healthy face by following healthy habits! Healthy habits mean you are healthy inside.

Eye Care Complete Guide for Sparkling Eyes

"Eyes express where words fail." "Eyes are the windows to your soul." These are just a couple of endless quotes about eyes. Eyes not only express your mind; they are also indicators of how healthy you are. Keeping your eyes healthy goes a long way toward maintaining a high confidence level.

Making Eye Creams

Eye Cream No. 1

Ingredients

Lemon essential oil or frankincense essential oil—20 drops

¼ cup aloe vera gel

¼ cup coconut oil

¼ cup shea butter

1 teaspoon vitamin E

Preparation

1. Heat the coconut oil and shea butter until they melt. Add all the ingredients to a bowl and mix well. Transfer the contents to a glass jar.

Eye Cream No. 2

Ingredients

Few slices cucumber

A handful mint leaves

4 teaspoons milk

4 teaspoons coconut oil or almond oil

¼ cup aloe vera gel

Preparation

1. Add the cucumber slices and mint leaves to a blender and blend well. Extract the juice and add the other ingredients. Mix well until you achieve a creamy consistency.

Natural Remedies for Puffy Eyes and Dark Circles

Puffy eyes and dark circles around the eyes have become common. While there are many reasons for puffy eyes, the most common cause is fluid retention. Dark circles around the eyes are generally caused by lack of sleep; other causes include sun exposure and allergies. Here are some of the best natural remedies for puffy eyes and dark circles under the eyes.

1) Cucumber

Cucumber is one of the most popular remedies to relieve tiredness of eyes and heal puffy eyes. It is a powerful antioxidant, and the flavonoids it contains cure swelling of the eyes.

Refrigerate two slices of cucumber until they are cool. Lie down and place one slice on each of your closed eyes. Remove it after 20 minutes.

2) Milk

Pour some cold milk in a bowl and dip a cotton ball into it. Squeeze the cotton ball to get rid of the excess milk and then place it on your eye. Place one on the other eye as well.

3) Potato

Potato possesses astringent properties and thus helps to extract fluid from under the eyes.

Take two slices of potato and place one on each eye. Remove after 20 minutes. Alternately, you can also grate the potato and make a poultice, which can be placed over the eyes.

4) Egg White

Egg white heals inflammation and promotes blood circulation.

Apply egg white under your eyes. Let it air dry. Remove it after 15 minutes and rinse with water.

5) Green or Black Tea

The caffeine in tea constricts micro blood vessels, and the tannins promote blood circulation, thereby addressing both puffy eyes and dark circles and tightening the skin under the eyes.

Dip two tea bags in a glass of hot water. Remove the bags after some time and let them cool to room temperature. Place the bags on your eyes for about half an hour.

6) Tomato

The lycopene in tomato keeps the skin softer and reduces dark circles around the eyes.

Add two teaspoons each of tomato juice and lemon juice to a bowl and mix well. Apply under the eyes. Wash off after 15 minutes.

7) Aloe Vera

Aloe vera has moisturizing properties. As an anti-inflammatory, it also reduces inflammation around the eyes.

Extract gel from an aloe vera leaf and apply it under the eyes. Gently massage for a few seconds. Rinse off after 15 minutes.

8) Turmeric

Turmeric possesses anti-aging properties. It tightens the skin around the eyes and prevents sagging.

Add some coconut oil to two teaspoons of turmeric to make a fine paste. Apply it under the eyes. Wash off after it dries.

9) Mint Leaves

Mint possesses astringent properties that constrict blood vessels. It also contains vitamin C that promotes glow. The menthol in mint leaves promotes blood circulation.

Make a paste from a handful of mint leaves. Apply it around the eyes. Rinse off after 15 minutes.

Tips for Eye Care

Prevention is better than cure. Taking care of your eyes the right way will ensure you have bright, sparkling eyes with no puffiness or dark circles. Here are some of the preventive measures you should adhere to:

- Get quality sleep. Sleep deprivation is a major cause for puffy eyes and dark circles. With a good night's sleep, you can make great progress.
- Eat a balanced diet in which fruits and vegetables are included.
- Stay hydrated. Drink plenty of water.
- Say "no" to caffeine.
- Wear sunglasses when you are out, even if the sun is not harsh.
- Take frequent breaks to look away from the computer screen so your eyes get some rest.
- Perform eye exercises regularly.

Caution

Never apply cream too close to your eyes. You want to avoid the risk of the cream getting into your eyes!

Before you try your homemade beauty product, do a patch test by applying the product to a small area of your hand. If you don't feel any allergic reactions, the product is safe for you to use.

Lip Care

Lips need a lot of attention, as they are prone to chapping and cracking. Whether it is summer or winter, lips gets more than their share of problems, and hence they require year-round care.

Making Lip Balms

Lip balms moisturize and protect the lips and heal chapped lips. As always with homemade products, making your own lip balms gives you the space to customize them to suit your lips and make your lips look the best.

Lip Balm No. 1

Ingredients
4 teaspoons honey
8 teaspoons almond oil
20 grams, about 1.4 tablespoons beeswax
30 grams, about 2 ¼ tablespoons shea butter
20 grams, about 1 ½ tablespoons cocoa butter

Preparation
1. Add the beeswax, shea butter and cocoa butter to a double boiler and melt them. Add the honey and almond oil and stir well. Blend well.

Lip Balm No. 2

Ingredients

10 drops lime essential oil

2 teaspoons almond oil

2 tablespoons coconut oil

2 teaspoons cocoa butter

2 teaspoons beeswax

Preparation

1. Place a double boiler over medium heat. Add the almond oil, coconut oil, cocoa butter and beeswax. Stir until the mixture melts. Remove from heat and add the lime essential oil. Mix well. Transfer to a container once cool.

Making Lip Scrubs

Lip scrubs exfoliate the lips and remove dryness. Using lip scrubs will keep your lips hydrated, soft and healthy.

Lip Scrub No. 1

Ingredients

Few drops honey

1 tablespoon brown sugar

1 to 2 drops vanilla

Preparation

1. Add the brown sugar to a bowl. Add the honey and vanilla and mix well. Store in a glass jar.

Lip Scrub No. 2

Ingredients

1 to 2 teaspoons coffee grounds

1 to 2 teaspoons honey

Preparation

1. Add the ingredients to a mixing bowl and mix well until they blend completely.

How to Make Lipsticks at Home

Lipsticks make the lips appear fuller and more attractive, boosting the wearer's confidence level about her appearance. A makeup kit is never complete without lipstick.

Lipstick No. 1

Ingredients

2 teaspoons beeswax

2 teaspoons shea butter

4 teaspoons sweet almond oil

2 teaspoons coconut oil

4 drops any essential oil

A pinch cocoa powder

Preparation

1. Add the shea butter and beeswax to a double boiler and melt them. Add the oils and cocoa powder and remove from heat. Add the essential oil and mix well. Store in a lipstick tube.

Lipstick No. 2

Ingredients

1 tablespoon olive oil

1 tablespoon beeswax

1 beetroot, dried and grated

Preparation

1. Melt the beeswax and olive oil in a double boiler. Slowly add the grated beetroot to the mixture as you keep stirring. Allow the lipstick to cool and then transfer to a container.

Natural Remedies for
Chapped, Dry, and Split Lips

Factors that can cause chapped lips include:

- Smoking
- Drinking
- Excessive licking of lips
- Sun exposure
- Dehydration
- Allergy
- Harsh weather

Split lips can be caused by harsh weather conditions, lip injuries, excessive licking of the lips, and dryness.

Given below are the best natural remedies to heal chapped and split lips:

1) Honey
The moisturizing and antibacterial properties of honey help to heal lips fast. Honey also retains moisture.

Apply a drop or two of honey to the lips. Repeat it several times a day until your lips improve.

2) Honey and Vaseline
Vaseline nourishes the lips and retains moisture. Using it along with honey can be very effective in treating chapped and split lips.

Apply honey to your lips, then apply Vaseline on top of the honey. Wipe off with a damp cloth after 15 minutes.

3) Coconut Oil

The moisturizing and lubricating properties of coconut oil help to keep your lips soft, prevent dryness, and heal cracks.

Add one to two drops of tea tree oil to two drops of coconut oil. Apply the mixture to your lips and leave it to be absorbed.

4) Cucumber

Cucumber hydrates the lips and prevents dryness.

Rub a cucumber slice on your lips for 1 minute. Rinse off after 10 minutes. Alternately, you can apply cucumber paste on your lips.

5) Butter

The essential fatty acids in butter hydrate the skin.

Apply some butter on your lips and massage gently. Leave it overnight.

6) Aloe Vera

Aloe vera has moisturizing properties. It keeps the lips moisturized and heals chapped lips.

Extract some gel from an aloe vera leaf. Apply the gel on your lips and massage gently. Leave it overnight.

7) Lemon Juice and Honey

Lemon exfoliates and bleaches the lips. Honey keeps the lips moisturized.

Mix together a teaspoon each of lemon juice and honey. Apply to your lips. Rinse after 10 to 15 minutes.

Natural Remedies for
Cold Sores on Lips

Cold sores, an infectious condition, can show up in any part of the body, but they generally occur on the lips, nose, cheeks and fingers. Though not serious, they can be painful. They can also be cured using natural remedies.

1) Lemon Balm
Lemon balm destroys the virus that causes cold sores.

Apply lemon balm to the affected area. Wash off after half an hour. Repeat once a day until the condition is cured.

2) Aloe Vera
Aloe vera is a potent antioxidant that fights infections and promotes healing.

Extract some gel from an aloe vera leaf and apply it to the sore. Leave it overnight.

3) Vanilla Oil
Vanilla oil possesses anti-inflammatory properties that cure infection and promote healing.

Dip a cotton ball in vanilla oil and apply it to the affected area. Wash off after a few minutes. Repeat until pain subsides and condition improves.

4) Garlic
The enzymes in garlic act as antiviral and antibacterial agents and aid in healing cold sores.

Crush a clove of garlic. Apply the crushed garlic to the cold sore. Rinse off after 10 minutes. Repeat 5 to 6 times a day.

5) Tea Tree Oil
The antiviral properties of tea tree oil support healing of cold sores.

Dilute a few drops of tea tree oil in water. Dip a small cotton ball in the diluted solution and apply it to the affected area. Leave it to dry. Repeat twice daily until symptoms improve.

Tips to Prevent Cold Sores

- Increase vitamin C intake.
- Increase intake of foods rich in zinc.
- Avoid stress triggers. Stress can raise the frequency of cold sores when the immune function is low.
- Stay away from spicy foods.
- Apply sunscreen.

Home Remedies to Lighten Dark Lips

The concerns about lips can be never-ending if you don't follow a healthy lifestyle. Cold sores, dry lips and dark lips can all be caused by poor immune system function due to an unhealthy lifestyle. Dark lips can result from dryness, excessive intake of coffee and tea, smoking, sun exposure, and reactions to certain cosmetics. Dark lips can be lightened using the following natural remedies.

1) Lemon Juice
Lemon contains vitamin C, which lightens dark lips. Lemon removes dead cells as well.

Add a teaspoon of sugar to the juice of half a lemon. Mix, apply to your lips and massage gently. Leave for about 15 minutes. Rinse off with water.

2) Coconut Oil
The essential fatty acids in coconut oil keep the lips hydrated, thereby lightening the lips.

Take two drops of coconut oil and apply it to your lips. Massage gently. Leave it on overnight.

3) Honey
Honey is a natural moisturizer. It also nourishes the lips and lightens dark lips.

Take some honey and apply it to your lips. Massage for a minute. Wash off after 15 to 20 minutes. You can also apply honey at night and leave it overnight.

4) Beetroot

Beetroot works great to remove a tan, and it's also effective for lightening dark lips.

Gently rub a slice of beetroot on your lips for a minute or two. Let it remain for about 15 minutes before washing it off.

5) Aloe Vera

The aloesin in aloe vera checks skin pigmentation and lightens the lips. It also nourishes the lips.

Apply aloe vera gel on the lips. Let it air dry before rinsing it off.

6) Baking Soda

Baking soda exfoliates the skin. Removal of dead cells helps to return the lips to their original color.

Add some water to baking soda to make a thick paste. Apply it to the lips. Scrub for a couple of minutes. Wash off and apply some coconut oil to your lips.

Lip Care in Summer and Winter

Rain or shine, your lips need care to keep them healthy and looking great. Here is how you go about it.

Summer Lip Care Tips

- Treat your lips with coconut oil every day. Massage the oil gently onto your lips and leave it to be absorbed.
- Eat balanced food that keeps your body hydrated.
- Increase your water intake. Drink lots of healthy juices.
- Apply lip balm to save your lips from exposure to the sun.
- Exfoliate your lips twice a week using honey and sugar or any other gentle method.
- Apply coconut oil to your lips before going to bed.

Winter Lip Care Tips

- Exfoliate your lips once or twice a week.
- Apply natural oils for moisturizing your lips.
- Apply butter to your lips.
- Massage your lips with ointment-based lip balm before sleep to prevent dryness.
- Avoid licking your lips.
- Do not scrub your lips when they are flaky.
- Treat cracked lips immediately.

Tooth Care
Keep Your Teeth
Sparkling Bright!

As it is popularly said, you don't have to brush all your teeth—just the ones you want to keep. A mouth without teeth can be hard to imagine and hard to swallow, mentally as well. The importance of oral hygiene can never be overstressed. From using the right toothpaste to taking care of teeth, you need to make wise choices to avoid sleepless nights with your hand on your cheek.

How to Make Toothpaste at Home

Do you worry about chemicals in your toothpaste every time you brush your teeth? If yes, you are already looking for a reliable alternative. And what could be better than your own homemade toothpaste?

Toothpaste No. 1

Ingredients

6 tablespoons coconut oil

6 tablespoons Bentonite clay

¾ teaspoon sea salt

10 to 12 drops peppermint or cinnamon or clove essential oil

¼ cup water

Preparation

1. Add the clay, coconut oil and salt to a mixing bowl. Mix the ingredients and add water little by little until the desired consistency is achieved. Add the essential oil and mix until the ingredients blend. Store the paste in an airtight container.

Toothpaste No. 2

Ingredients

6 tablespoons coconut oil

3 teaspoons bentonite clay

¼ cup baking soda

6 teaspoons calcium magnesium powder

15 drops peppermint essential oil

10 to 12 drops trace minerals

Preparation

1. Melt the coconut oil in a double boiler. Remove from heat. Add the remaining ingredients and mix well. Transfer to a container and refrigerate for a few minutes until the paste thickens.

Natural Remedies to Whiten Your Teeth

Stained, discolored teeth can make your laughter much less charming. There is more to it, though. Your teeth represent your level of hygiene, so it's important to keep them white and sparkling. Here are some of the best home remedies for whitening your teeth.

1) Baking Soda
Baking soda fights bacteria and minimizes the risk of tooth decay.

Brush your teeth gently with baking soda.

2) Oil Pulling
There are many benefits associated with oil pulling, and dental health is very much included. Coconut oil, which is generally used for oil pulling, kills bacteria, prevents tooth decay and reduces inflammation.

Swish a teaspoon of coconut oil around inside your mouth for about 20 minutes. Spit it out and rinse your mouth well with water.

3) Hydrogen Peroxide
Hydrogen peroxide bleaches your teeth and removes stains. It also destroys bacteria on your teeth.

To avoid the risk of overusing hydrogen peroxide, mix it with baking soda in a 2:1 ratio to brush your teeth.

Using the above-mentioned remedies to whiten your teeth and maintain oral hygiene goes a long way toward preventing your teeth from getting yellow. Here are a few basics to adhere to:

- Brush your teeth twice a day.
- Floss your teeth every day.
- Increase your intake of calcium-rich foods.
- Limit your intake of sugar and beverages such as coffee and soda.
- Quit smoking.
- Avoid chewing tobacco.

Neck Care

Postpone Aging

Symptoms!

The most often ignored part of the body is the neck—that is, until it starts hurting! The neck is given far less attention than the face, hair or even the fingernails. Nevertheless, neck wrinkles are telltale signs of aging, and a dark neck shows that you haven't been paying enough attention to neck care.

How to Make Neck Cream at Home

First of all, why do you need neck cream when you can use face cream on your neck? Well, using neck-specific creams is more beneficial because neck skin is thinner than face skin and has a different cellular composition. Furthermore, there are fewer sebaceous glands in your neck, so oil secretion is less, meaning that aging symptoms appear faster. That should be reason enough to use creams specifically made for the neck!

Neck Cream

Ingredients
3 tablespoons beeswax
1½ to 2 cups almond oil
2 teaspoons frankincense oil
½ to ¾ cup calendula oil
1½ teaspoons lemon oil

Preparation
1. Melt the beeswax in a double boiler. Remove from heat and add all the oils. Mix well to form a paste. Transfer the cream to a container.

Home Remedies for Neck Wrinkles

A sagging neck does your appearance no favors. Here are the best home remedies to treat neck wrinkles.

1) Egg White
Egg white not only tightens your skin—it also brightens your skin.

Whip one egg white well. Add a teaspoon of honey. Mix well to blend. Apply the paste to your neck and leave it for about half an hour.

2) Pineapple
Pineapple promotes skin elasticity and prevents wrinkle formation.

Apply pineapple juice to your neck and massage in an upward motion for 2 to 3 minutes. Rinse off with cold water after 10 minutes.

3) Coconut Oil
Being a rich source of antioxidants, coconut oil repairs collagen and promotes neck health. Coconut oil moisturizes the skin and prevents wrinkle formation due to skin dryness.

Apply coconut oil to your neck, massage gently, and leave it to be absorbed.

4) Tomato
Tomato promotes skin regeneration and a youthful appearance.

Add some turmeric powder to some tomato juice and mix well. Apply it to your neck and let it air dry. Rinse off with water.

5) Shea Butter
Shea butter moisturizes the skin and prevents dryness and wrinkles. It increases collagen production. It is also anti-inflammatory.

Home Remedies to Treat Dark Neck

If your neck is not as good as your face, it only shows that you have not attended to your neck as much as you have attended to your face. Try these home remedies to address dark neck.

1) Turmeric
Turmeric improves skin tone and also possesses anti-inflammatory properties that aid in healing the skin.

Add some turmeric to yogurt and make a paste. Apply it to your neck. Rinse off after 15 minutes.

2) Oats
Oats are a great cleanser and moisturizer. Scrubbing with oats helps to remove dead skin cells and promote skin health.

Coarsely powder some oats and add some tomato juice. Mix well to make a paste. Apply to your neck. Scrub your neck gently after 15 minutes. Rinse off with water.

3) Potato
Potato bleaches the skin, removes dark patches and promotes better skin tone.

Extract the juice from one potato. Apply it to your neck and let it air dry. Rinse off after 15 minutes.

4) Aloe Vera
Aloe vera hydrates the skin. It prevents excessive skin pigmentation and improves skin tone.

Extract gel from an aloe vera leaf and apply it to your neck. Wash it off after 15 to 20 minutes.

5) *Baking Soda*

Baking soda exfoliates the skin, boosts circulation, and removes tans.

Add some water to some baking soda to make a smooth paste. Apply it to your neck and let it air dry. Wet your fingertips and scrub your neck gently. Rinse with water.

Hair Care
A Woman's Treasure

Next to the face, it is the hair that gets the most attention. Thinning of hair, graying of hair and do-it-yourself herbal shampoos top Google searches for a reason. A perfect hair style complements your looks, but it is possible to achieve only if you enjoy super hair health. Fortunately, from making shampoos to treating hair loss and graying of hair, you can do everything from the comfort of your home—and the best part is that it is customized hair care.

Making Shampoo at Home

Shampooing removes the dirt that has accumulated in your hair and gets rid of excess oil. You should therefore shampoo your hair 2 to 3 times a week depending on your hair type.

Hair Shampoo No. 1

Ingredients
½ cup coconut milk
½ cup liquid castile soap
40 drops lavender essential oil

Preparation
1. Add all the ingredients to a bowl and mix well. Transfer the contents to a shampoo bottle. Shake well before each use.

Hair Shampoo No. 2

Ingredients

1 cup coconut milk

2 tablespoons honey

1 teaspoon castor oil

1 teaspoon rosemary essential oil

2 tablespoons apple cider vinegar

Preparation

1. Add all the ingredients to a mixing bowl and mix well. Transfer to a container. Shake well before use.

How to Make Hair Conditioner at Home

Hair conditioner keeps your hair tangle-free, smooth and shiny. Moisture, which is stripped when you shampoo your hair, is replenished by hair conditioner. Conditioner checks hair breaks and supports hair growth.

Hair Conditioner No. 1

Ingredients
2 tablespoons coconut oil
2 tablespoons lemon juice
2 tablespoons honey
2 tablespoons curd
1 tablespoon essential oil

Preparation
1. Making curd: Boil one glass of milk. Remove from heat and let cool to lukewarm. Add ¼ teaspoon of store-bought curd or two teaspoons of lemon juice to the warm milk and mix with a spoon. Set aside for 5 to 6 hours during summer and for more than 9 hours during winter. Your curd is ready for use after the specified time.
2. Add all the ingredients to a mixing bowl and mix thoroughly. Apply to your hair after shampooing. Rinse off after 15 minutes.

Hair Conditioner 2

Ingredients
5 tablespoons aloe vera
1 tablespoon lemon juice

Preparation
1. Add the ingredients to a bowl and mix well. Apply to your shampooed hair. Rinse off with water after 10 minutes.

Hair Mask for Hair Growth

A hair mask could be the best thing to happen to your hair! A hair mask strengthens, nourishes and hydrates your hair to keep it soft and shining.

Hair Mask No. 1

Ingredients
1 ripe banana
1 tablespoon olive oil or coconut oil

Preparation
1. Grind a ripe banana to a smooth paste. Add the oil and blend well. Apply to wet hair. Leave it for 15 minutes. Rinse off with water.

Hair Mask No. 2

Ingredients
1 tablespoon coconut oil
1 tablespoon honey
1 teaspoon cinnamon

Preparation
1. Add all the ingredients to a mixing bowl. Mix well. Apply to your hair. Rinse off after 15 to 20 minutes.

Natural Remedies for Hair Growth

Hair loss can be effectively treated at home using natural remedies. Here are the best home remedies for hair growth.

1) Onion Juice
Studies prove the effect of onion juice in promoting hair growth. The sulfur in onions boosts production of collagen and supports hair growth.

Slice a big red onion and blend it well. Filter the juice and apply it to your scalp. Massage gently for a couple of minutes. Rinse off with water and a mild shampoo after half an hour. You can apply onion juice 3 to 4 times a week for quick results.

2) Potato Juice
Potato is a rich source of zinc, iron, starch, vitamin B and vitamin C. It extracts excess oil, cleanses hair follicles, prevents hair breakage and promotes hair growth.

Extract the juice from one or two potatoes. Apply it to your scalp and massage gently for a couple of minutes. Rinse with mild shampoo after half an hour. Potato juice can be applied on your scalp 4 times a week.

3) Turmeric
Turmeric possesses anti-inflammatory properties and is effective for treating scalp infections. It gets rid of dandruff and promotes hair growth.

Add about ¼ cup of turmeric to one cup of milk. Add some honey and mix well so the ingredients blend. Apply to your scalp. Rinse off after half an hour with mild shampoo.

4) Carrot

Carrot is a rich source of minerals and vitamins. Being a potent antioxidant, it heals hair follicles and promotes hair growth.

Grate a carrot. Apply it to your scalp. You can also extract carrot juice and apply that to your scalp. Wash your hair with shampoo after 20 minutes.

5) Curry Leaves

Being a rich source of iron, calcium and vitamins, curry leaves not only postpone graying of hair but also promote hair growth.

Add one cup of tightly packed curry leaves to one cup of coconut oil. Place over medium heat and remove from heat after a black residue forms. Strain the oil after it cools down. Apply it to your scalp and massage for 2 to 3 minutes. Rinse off with shampoo after one hour.

Natural Remedies to Reverse Prematurely Gray Hair and Postpone Graying of Hair As You Age

While it is not possible to completely get rid of the gray hair that comes with age, it is possible to bring it to its natural color through constant use of homemade remedies. And the remedies work perfectly for those whose hair goes gray while they're still young.

1) Curry Leaves
As mentioned above, curry leaves are effective in reversing gray hair because they are a rich source of iron, calcium and vitamins.

Add one cup of tightly packed curry leaves to one cup of coconut oil and place it over medium heat. Remove from heat after a black residue forms. Cool the mixture. Strain and apply it to your scalp and hair. Massage for a couple of minutes. Rinse off with shampoo after one hour.

2) Amla
A very rich source of vitamin C and a potent antioxidant, amla is one of the best solutions for hair health.

Extract the juice from one amla and add a tablespoon of coconut oil to it. Blend well. (You can use a double boiler to melt the oil, if needed.) Massage the freshly made amla oil on your scalp and hair. Rinse off with shampoo after one hour.

3) Black Tea
The caffeine in black tea is a powerful antioxidant that works great for promoting hair health. Black tea also improves the color of hair and promotes shine.

Bring a cup of water to boil and add about 2 tablespoons of black tea. Simmer for a couple of seconds and turn off the heat. Let it cool. Apply it to your scalp and hair and let it air dry. Rinse off after half an hour.

4) Sage Leaves

The antioxidant properties of sage leaves help to prevent graying of hair. Sage oil strengthens hair roots and moisturizes the hair. The natural pigments in sage oil bring gray hair to its normal color with regular use.

Add one handful of sage leaves to a glass of water and bring to a boil. Reduce the heat, cover the pot and simmer for 5 minutes. Turn off the heat and let the sage tea cool. Filter and apply to your scalp and hair. Rinse off after two hours.

5) Potato Peels

Potato peels contain starch, which adds pigment to gray hair and returns the hair to its natural color.

Add two cups of water to ½ cup of potato peels. Bring to a boil and boil until a thick, starchy solution forms. Remove from heat and let cool. Strain the liquid. Wash your hair and apply the liquid on your scalp and hair. Do not rinse.

Nail Care
How to Make
Your Nails Glow

Did you know that nails talk? Yes, and they speak the truth! While naturally glowing nails reflect how healthy you are, broken, brittle and discolored nails are signs of ill health and malnutrition. Having a balanced diet and getting a good night's sleep every day play a vital role in supporting nail health. While you are working at improving your lifestyle, you can also keep your nails healthy and glowing with DIY nail products and home remedies.

How to Make 100% Chemical-Free Nail Polish

If you love nail polish but hate the fact that the nail polish sold in the supermarket is loaded with chemicals, here is some great news for you: You can make nail polish at home that is 100% chemical-free. Here you go.

Nail Polish No. 1

Ingredients

6 tablespoons olive oil

5 teaspoons ginger root powder (alternatively, you can use 4 teaspoons of alkanet root powder for red color and 4 teaspoons of charcoal for dark gray color)

¾ teaspoon beeswax

¾ teaspoon frankincense or jojoba essential oil

4 drops vitamin E oil

Preparation

1. Add the olive oil to a pan and place it over low heat. While stirring the oil, add the ginger or alkanet root powder. Add the beeswax and let it melt. Add the other oils and mix well until the ingredients blend. Transfer the nail polish to a container.

Homemade Nail Polish Remover

As you'd expect, the nail polish removers sold in the supermarket are full of harsh chemicals. Just as when you make your own nail polish at home, making your own nail polish remover will help you stay chemical-free.

1) Lemon

Dip your fingers in warm water for a few minutes. Once your nail polish starts softening, remove your fingers from the water and rub a cut lemon on the nails to remove your nail polish.

2) Nail Polish

Strange as it may sound, you will find the results effective. The fresh nail polish you apply over the existing one will dissolve the dried nail polish. Just use any nail polish to get the job done.

3) Vinegar and Lemon

Extract the juice from one lemon and add some vinegar to it. Mix well. Dip your fingers in it for about 1 minute. Take your fingers out and gently rub your nails with a cotton ball. After removing the nail polish, wash your hands with water.

Home Remedies to
Remove Nail Fungus

Nail fungus is generally caused by fungal or yeast infections. Other causes include compromised immune function, poor circulation, and damaged nail beds; in some cases, it can be genetic. With the right remedies, you can cure nail fungus at home regardless of how long you have been experiencing the condition.

1) Balanced Diet
This is where you need to start if you want to eliminate the cause completely. Increase your intake of protein, iron, calcium and fiber. Drink vegetable juice. Include garlic, chia seeds and turmeric in your diet. Avoid sugar and grains. Maintain a record of foods that cause allergic reactions and avoid them.

2) Tea Tree Oil
Tea tree oil has antiseptic and antifungal properties that aid in curing nail fungus.

Wash the affected nails with water and dry them. Apply tea tree oil directly on the nails. Gently scrub the affected nails after 10 to 15 minutes.

3) Olive Leaf Extract
Olive leaf extract possesses antifungal and antiviral properties. It is also an immune booster and hence is effective in treating nail fungus.

Apply olive leaf extract to the fungus-affected nails. Let it be absorbed. You can also consume olive leaf capsules twice daily.

4) Oregano Essential Oil

The antifungal, antibacterial and anti-inflammatory properties of oregano oil help to treat nail fungus.

Simply apply oregano essential oil to the affected nails.

5) Baking Soda

Baking soda prevents the growth of fungus by soaking up moisture.

Make a paste of baking soda and water. Apply it to the affected nails and rinse off after 15 minutes.

Hand Care
Never Let Your Hands
Let You Down

Your hands can give away your age if you don't pay them the attention you pay your face. Wrinkles in your hands and fingers are very revealing. Considering the fact that your hands are most exposed to ultraviolet rays, water, chemicals you use in household chores and so on, it is essential that they be given due attention. Here is how to attend to your hands so they are healthy, wrinkle-free and youthful.

Make Your Hand Creams at Home

Hand creams moisturize your hands, prevent damage to skin, and keep your hands soft.

Hand Cream No. 1

Ingredients
¼ cup, grated beeswax
2 cups olive oil
15 to 20 drops tea tree or lavender essential oil

Preparation
1. Add the beeswax and olive oil to a double boiler on the stove. Stir until the beeswax melts. Remove from heat. Add the essential oil. Mix well so the ingredients blend. Store in an airtight container.

Hand Cream No. 2

Ingredients

6 teaspoons shea butter

1 tablespoon coconut oil

10 to 12 drops lavender essential oil

5 drops peppermint essential oil

Preparation

1. Add the shea butter to a double boiler on the stove. After the shea butter melts, add the coconut oil. Remove from heat and add the essential oils. Mix well. Refrigerate until the cream solidifies.

Simple Hand Scrubs to Make at Home

Hand scrubs exfoliate dead skin cells, make your hands soft and promote a youthful appearance.

1) Sugar
Add two teaspoons of sugar to a teaspoon of olive oil or coconut oil. Mix well. Apply to your hands and fingers. Scrub for a couple of minutes. Rinse well after 10 minutes.

2) Oatmeal
Oatmeal removes dead skin cells and makes your hands soft.

Add 2 teaspoons of oatmeal to a mixing bowl along with 1 teaspoon each of baking soda and sea salt. Mix well. Add some water to make a paste. Apply it to your hands and fingers. Scrub gently for a couple of minutes. Rinse well after 10 minutes.

How To Keep Your Hands and Fingers Wrinkle-Free

Your hands and fingers should be given as much care as you give your face. Keeping your hands and fingers wrinkle-free gives you a youthful appearance and greatly increases your confidence.

1) Banana
Bananas seem to have a role in keeping every part of your body glowing and healthy. Being a rich source of minerals and vitamins and having excellent moisturizing properties, bananas

are an absolutely great solution for keeping your hands and fingers wrinkle-free.

Mash a ripe banana and make a paste. Apply it to your hands and fingers. Leave it for about 20 minutes and rinse well.

2) Rice Water

Rice water is a powerful antioxidant and a great source of vitamins and minerals. It minimizes the pores, tightens your skin, and keeps your skin wrinkle-free.

Rice water can be made with uncooked or cooked rice.

- **Rice Water from Uncooked Rice**—Add ½ cup of rice to a bowl and rinse well until it is free of impurities. Add 2 cups of pure water to the rice and let it soak for about 20 minutes. Strain the rice and collect the water in a bowl.
- **Rice Water from Cooked Rice**—Cook rice as you normally do. Strain the excess water and store it for future use.

Apply rice water to your hands and fingers. Leave it to dry for about 20 minutes. Rinse well with tap water.

3) Coconut Oil

Coconut oil promotes collagen production, thereby aiding in the regeneration of skin cells. Thus, it prevents wrinkles and promotes youthfulness.

Apply coconut oil to your hands and fingers. Massage for a couple of minutes. Let the oil be absorbed by your skin.

4) Lemon and Sugar

Lemon removes age spots and sugar exfoliates dead skin cells and softens your hands. Combining them will provide optimum benefits.

Add one or two teaspoons of sugar to the juice of one lemon. Mix well and apply it to your hands and fingers. Gently scrub for a few seconds and leave it to dry. Rinse well after 15 minutes.

5) Aloe Vera

The health benefits of aloe vera are immense; so are its beauty benefits. Aloe vera is a great moisturizer and is also effective in promoting skin elasticity and thereby preventing wrinkles.

Extract aloe vera gel from a fresh aloe leaf. Apply the gel to your hands and fingers. Rinse well after 20 minutes.

Foot Care
Walk Your Feet to Beauty

It goes without saying that your face gets the most attention when you are getting ready for an outing. Yet your beauty is complete only when your feet are healthy and beautiful. Give your feet the best care. After all, they are the ones that carry your weight and take you places.

Making Foot Cream

Applying foot cream prevents dryness and keeps your feet hydrated. Foot cream keeps your feet soft and glowing.

Foot Cream No. 1

Ingredients
½ cup shea butter
6 teaspoons, grated beeswax
¼ cup coconut oil
¼ cup olive oil
16 drops lavender essential oil
16 drops lemon essential oil

Preparation
1. Add the shea butte and beeswax to a double boiler and place it over heat. Add the coconut oil and olive oil and keep stirring until the ingredients melt. Remove from heat and let cool. Add the essential oils and mix well until the ingredients blend. Transfer to a container.

Foot Cream No. 2

Ingredients

1 cup honey

2 tablespoons milk

Orange juice from ½ orange

Preparation

1. Warm the honey and milk and stir them well. Add the orange juice to the mixture. Blend well and store in an air-tight container.

Homemade Foot Soaks

Foot soaks hydrate and soothe your skin. They cure muscle soreness, relieve pain and reduce swelling.

1) Basic Foot Soak
Add a handful of sea salt to enough water to soak your feet in. Heat until the water is hot enough for you. Pour the hot water into a tub. Place your feet in it for about 15 minutes. Remove your feet from the water and pat them dry.

2) Lemon and Honey
Add the juice of half a lemon and about 2 to 3 tablespoons of honey to some hot water. Soak your feet in it for about 15 minutes. Remove your feet and pat dry.

3) Epsom Salt
Add one cup of Epsom salt to some hot water and let it dissolve. Soak your feet in the water for about 15 minutes. Remove your feet from the water and pat them dry.

4) Essential Oils
Add few drops of essential oil to hot water and soak your feet in it. The following essential oils are some of the best for the indicated foot conditions.

- Lavender essential oil—Relieves pain
- Peppermint essential oil—Promotes cellular regeneration and purifies the skin
- Eucalyptus essential oil—Relieves fatigue and hydrates the feet
- Tea tree essential oil—Heals wounds and fungal infections
- Olive oil—Heals wounds

How to Soften
Rough Heels Naturally

Rough and cracked heels are caused by various factors including dryness, skin conditions, obesity and prolonged hours of standing on hard surfaces. Rough heels are also seen in those with diabetes and thyroid conditions. Here are some of the best home remedies to treat rough heels.

1) Coconut Oil
The moisturizing properties of coconut oil can keep your heels soft. Coconut oil also possesses antifungal properties and hence is effective in improving skin conditions.

Apply coconut oil on your feet and massage for a couple of minutes. Leave it to be absorbed by your skin. The ideal time to apply it would be after a foot soak and just before bed.

2) Lemon
Lemon is acidic in nature, which helps to remove dead cells from the feet.

Soak your feet in a tub of warm water containing lemon juice. Remove your feet after 10 to 15 minutes and scrub gently to exfoliate the skin.

3) Epsom Salt
The magnesium in Epsom salt detoxifies the skin and promotes skin health, thereby addressing rough heels.

Add ½ cup of Epsom salt to a tub filled with warm water. Soak your feet in it. Remove them after about 10 minutes and scrub gently. Rinse and pat dry. Apply coconut oil to your feet.

4) Rice Flour

Place some coarse rice flour in a mixing bowl. Add one teaspoon each of honey, coconut oil or olive oil and apple cider vinegar and mix well to make a thick paste. Apply the paste to your feet and massage gently. Rinse off after 15 minutes. Apply moisturizer on your feet.

5) Banana

Banana is a natural moisturizer that promotes skin softness.

Mash a ripe banana in a blender to make a thick paste. Apply it to your feet and let it remain for about 15 minutes. Wash off with water and pat dry.

Foot Care Tips

Here are the most essential rules you need to follow to keep your feet healthy.

- Wash your feet every time you return home from outside. Apart from that, wash them regularly in the morning and at night.
- Never forget to dry your feet after washing.
- Moisturize your feet to prevent dryness.
- Apply sunscreen before setting out.
- Exfoliate your feet twice or thrice a week.
- Massage your feet with oil every day.
- Trim your toenails.
- Use foot packs and foot soaks twice or thrice a week.
- Wear well-fitting shoes.
- Wash your socks every day.

Body Care
For a Perfect Body

Who wouldn't love to have a perfect body that goes well with the wildest imaginable outfits? Having an enviably flat tummy is not all there is to it. You also need to care for your body the way you care for your face. Yes, you got it right—scrubs, body wash, anything and everything you make at home for your face, you should also make for your body.

Making Body Wash at Home

Unlike soap, body wash does not dry your skin. Body wash cleanses and moisturizes your body, leaving your skin soft.

Body Wash No. 1

Ingredients
1 cup liquid castile soap
1 cup honey
¼ cup olive oil
¼ cup castor oil
20 drops frankincense or geranium essential oil

Preparation
1. Add the liquid castile soap to a container. Add the honey and all the oils. Shake well and use.

Body Wash No. 2

Ingredients

½ cup liquid castile soap

¾ cup coconut milk

2 teaspoons honey

3 teaspoons glycerin

4 teaspoons jojoba essential oil

12 drops lavender essential oil

Preparation

1. Add the coconut milk and liquid castile soap to a bottle. Add the remaining ingredients and mix well by shaking with the lid closed.

How to Make Body Scrubs at Home

Body scrubs are effective in exfoliating dead cells. Exfoliating your skin twice a week helps to achieve healthy and glowing skin.

1) Coconut Oil and Sugar
Add 2 to 3 tablespoons of sugar to ¼ cup of coconut oil. You can also add 2 to 3 drops of an essential oil of your choice. Mix well. Apply to your skin. Massage gently on each part of your body. Wash off after scrubbing.

2) Sea Salt and Brown Sugar
Take equal amounts of sea salt and brown sugar and add coconut oil to form a paste. Apply it to your body and scrub gently for a few minutes. Wash off after scrubbing.

Homemade Body Sprays
Fragrance Perfect

Wearing body spray brings feelings of freshness. The fresh scent from naturally-made body sprays lasts for many hours. Just imagine the level of freshness and happiness you will experience when you use your handmade body spray!

Body Spray No. 1

Ingredients

2 tablespoons witch hazel

50 drops any essential oil

2 cups distilled water

Preparation

1. Add all ingredients to a spray container. Seal and shake the container well.

Body Spray No. 2

Ingredients

20 drops sandalwood essential oil

2 teaspoons rosewater

Preparation

1. Add both the ingredients to a spray bottle. Seal the bottle and shake well.

Make Your Own Deodorants

The difference between deodorants and body sprays is mainly in the concentration of essential oil, which is higher in body spray than in deodorant. Using natural deodorants saves you from the side effects associated with store-bought deodorants.

Deodorant No. 1

Ingredients
2 tablespoons baking soda
1½ tablespoons shea butter
2 tablespoons coconut oil
2 to 3 drops tea tree essential oil

Preparation
1. Add the shea butter and coconut oil to a double boiler and place it over heat. Remove from heat after the ingredients melt. Add the baking soda. Mix well until the ingredients blend. Add the tea tree essential oil and mix well. Store in a container.

Deodorant No. 2

Ingredients
5 drops lemon essential oil
5 drops grapefruit essential oil
5 drops sage essential oil
5 drops peppermint essential oil
5 drops rosemary essential oil
2 tablespoons coconut oil

Preparation
1. Mix all the ingredients well until they blend. Store in a container.

Making Hair Remover at Home

Even those who can do without other cosmetic items will have a hair remover at home. Not that there are any health benefits associated with removing body hair. It's simply that, over the course of time, women have been made to believe that a hairless body is beautiful—and that female body hair is not socially acceptable. Women who have a lot of body hair—either because they prefer it that way or because they just don't want to bother getting rid of it—have been considered arrogant, unattractive, and unacceptable in the upper reaches of society. However, we must stress that hair removal is not mandatory; it is an individual preference. And if you prefer not to have hair, it is best done using natural hair remover made at home.

1) Sugar Wax

Place 1¼ cups of sugar in a bowl and add 5 tablespoons each of lemon juice and water. Place over medium heat and stir continuously while bringing to a boil. Reduce the heat and simmer for a few minutes, still stirring constantly. Remove from heat when the mixture changes to a golden brown color. Let it cool before transferring the sugar wax to a jar.

Apply the wax to the area where you want to remove hair. Wait for a minute. Lift the corner of the applied sugar wax and rip off in the direction opposite to hair growth. Cleanse the area with water.

2) Egg White

Add 1 tablespoon of sugar and ½ tablespoon of corn flour to one egg white. Mix well until the ingredients blend. Apply a thin layer to the area where you want to remove excess hair. Leave it for about 20 minutes. Peel off the mask and rinse the area with water.

Full-Body Clay Mask

This is not a modern invention; clay has been used for face and body masks since ancient times. Ancient cultures used clay for treating various health conditions, including skin problems. Bentonite clay, one of the most common types used by the ancients, possesses a strong negative electromagnetic charge, which draws metals and toxins out from the body when the clay is applied to the skin.

Take about 1 cup of Bentonite clay and add sufficient water to make a paste. Apply it to your body and face. Shower after 15 minutes. You can also pour the paste in your tub, swirl the water well, and soak in it.

Perfect and Relaxing Bath
Have a Whale of a Time!

Routine bathing certainly has its benefits, but it doesn't offer the pleasures and fun of a perfect bath prepared with creativity and care. If your weekday bathing consists entirely of two-minute showers, you owe it to yourself to unwind in a relaxing bath on weekends! Here, let us see how to prepare a bath that is relaxing, rejuvenating, energizing, unwinding and anything else you can dream of.

Set the Ambiance

Start with the basics. You have waited all week long for this perfect bath, so ambiance matters. Place candles around the bathroom; you're sure to love the calm of candlelit bathing. If you are a book or music lover—or both—here is an opportunity to indulge in your passion. Create a bathtub caddy and stock it with a few books on your bucket list, a music player loaded with your favorite songs, and maybe a coffee cup or a wineglass. Buy a bath pillow to support your neck while you take a long, relaxing bath.

The Bath Itself

The highlight of preparing your bath is customizing it to suit your tastes and needs.

- Epsom salt soak and lemongrass for relaxing your muscles
- Lavender and ylang ylang essential oil to relax your mind
- Eucalyptus essential oil to decongest
- Geranium essential oil to calm your mind
- Peppermint, geranium and lavender essential oils to relieve stress
- Lemon, thyme and bergamot essential oils to energize you

Rules to Follow, Naturally

Every procedure has its rules, and using essential oils in your bath is no exception. Here are the points to note for a safe and effective essential oil bath:

- Never add essential oil directly to your bath. Mix essential oil with a carrier oil of your choice in the ratio of 12 drops of essential oil to 1 tablespoon of carrier oil. Once it is thoroughly mixed, add it to your bathtub and swirl so the essential oil is evenly dispersed in the water.
- Add essential oil after your bathtub is full.
- Choose your essential oil with care. Regardless of your preference for a particular essential oil, check to make sure that it's skin-friendly. For your bathtub, you need an essential oil that soothes and supports your skin health.

Pregnancy Skin Care

Pregnancy is the most wonderful phase in a woman's life. Taking the best care of your baby in the womb is the experience of a lifetime, one that words can never describe. However, it also involves dealing with hormonal changes that can cause skin conditions such as itchy skin and acne. While it is always essential that you use natural methods to keep your skin healthy, during pregnancy you need to be doubly sure of what you are applying to your skin—just as sure as you are about what you put in your mouth.

The most common skin conditions associated with pregnancy are:

- Itchy skin
- Pigmentation
- Dark circles
- Stretch marks
- Acne
- Varicose veins

Natural Remedies for Itchy Skin During Pregnancy

Itchy skin is common in pregnant women. Here is what you can do to treat itching during pregnancy.

- Apply coconut oil or almond oil on itchy areas.
- Apply aloe vera gel.
- Use moisturizing shower gel.
- Apply natural moisturizer after showering.
- Apply calamine lotion.
- Add two teaspoons of baking soda to your bath.
- Add one cup of oatmeal to your bath and soak for about 10 minutes.

Natural Remedies for
Pigmentation During Pregnancy

Pigmentation is the occurrence of dark patches or spots on the skin. It is caused by an increase in melanin during pregnancy. Pigmentation is generally found on the forehead, cheeks and neck.

- Wear loose-fitting clothes.
- Do not use chemicals on your skin.
- Add one to two teaspoons of oats to some honey and make a paste. Apply it to the affected areas and gently exfoliate. Rinse well and moisturize.
- Extract some gel from an aloe vera leaf and apply it to the affected area. Rinse off after 10 to 15 minutes.
- Mix juices of lemon and cucumber and apply to the affected parts.

Natural Remedies for
Dark Circles During Pregnancy

Hormonal changes, sleep deprivation, fluid retention and hyperpigmentation are some factors that cause dark circles in pregnant women. While this is naturally reversed after delivery, there are quite a few things you can do to improve it while you are still pregnant.

- Get quality sleep every day. Avoid using electronic gadgets for at least an hour before you go to bed.
- Increase your water intake.
- Eat a balanced diet that gives you your share of nutrients.
- Apply coconut oil or raw almond oil under your eyes before bed.
- Extract the juice from a cucumber. Dip a cotton ball into the juice and apply it to the dark circles. Rinse off after 10 to 15 minutes. You can also add lemon juice in equal proportion to the cucumber juice.
- Apply juice made from mint leaves to the dark circles. Rinse off after 10 to 15 minutes.
- Meditate regularly to stay stress-free; stress can contribute to skin conditions.
- Refrigerate some used green tea bags. Apply one to each of the dark circles. Remove after 15 minutes.
- Place cold towels on your eyes. You can also apply cold milk under your eyes.

Natural Remedies for Stretch Marks

Stretch marks generally occur in the later stages of pregnancy, although in some cases they may be seen as soon as the bump begins to form. Your chances of getting stretch marks are higher if they run in your family. Other causes include rapid weight gain and getting pregnant at a young age. Here is how you can minimize the appearance of stretch marks.

- Increase your intake of foods rich in vitamin C.
- Increase your water intake.
- Apply coconut oil on your tummy to keep your skin moisturized and prevent stretch marks.
- Use castor oil, shea butter and cocoa butter on your tummy so your skin is hydrated. You can also apply aloe vera gel to make the stretch marks fade.
- Apply honey to the stretch marks. Honey moisturizes the skin and improves skin tone. Rinse off after 15 to 20 minutes.
- Take equal amounts of turmeric and sandalwood powder. Add some water to make a paste. Apply it to the stretch marks. Rinse off after 15 minutes.

Natural Remedies for
Acne During Pregnancy

Acne outbreaks are common during the early months of pregnancy because increased oil production due to hormonal changes results in clogging of pores. Here are some natural remedies you can use to treat acne during pregnancy.

- Apply coconut oil to acne-affected areas before going to bed. Leave it overnight to be absorbed by the skin.
- Apply lemon juice to the affected area. Rinse off after 10 minutes.
- Take ½ teaspoon of turmeric and add some water to make a paste. Apply to the affected area. Rinse off after 30 to 40 minutes.
- Apply honey to the affected area. Rinse off after 30 minutes.
- Mash a papaya and blend it to make a paste. Apply it to the affected skin. Rinse off after 10 minutes.
- Apply aloe vera gel to the affected area. Rinse off after 30 minutes.
- Apply tea tree oil on acne-affected areas before you go to sleep at night. Let it be absorbed by the skin.
- Add honey to some cooked oatmeal to form a paste. Rub it gently on the affected area and rinse after 15 minutes.

Also remember:

- Drink at least 12 glasses of water every day.
- Cleanse your face in the morning and at night before bed. Also cleanse after coming back home from outside.
- Never scratch the affected area.
- Get enough sleep to support immune function and hormone balance.
- Shampoo your hair regularly to prevent it from getting oily.
- Avoid using chemical cosmetics.

Natural Remedies for Varicose Veins During Pregnancy

Varicose veins occur in some pregnant women. Various factors contribute to the condition, including hormonal changes and poor blood flow from the legs to the pelvis causing pressure in the veins. It also runs in the family. Here is how you can treat varicose veins naturally at home:

- Exercise regularly. Perform yoga poses that are recommended for pregnant women.
- Avoid prolonged hours of sitting or standing. When sitting, do not let your legs hang down. Elevate your legs and place them on a stool.
- Do not sit cross legged as this can pressurize the veins.
- Sleep on your left side to promote blood flow to the whole body.
- Do not wear tight fitting clothes that may inhibit proper circulation.
- Do not wear heels.
- Increase your water intake.
- Eat foods that are rich in vitamin C, fiber and magnesium.
- Add garlic juice to olive oil and mix well. Let the mixture sit for 12 hours. Apply it to the affected area when you go to bed. (You can wrap some cotton around it so it won't stain your sheets.)
- Apply rose essential oil to the affected area to cure itching.
- Watch your weight. Maintaining a healthy weight goes a long way toward preventing varicose veins.

In spite of certain problems associated with pregnancy, it's the most wonderful experience a woman can ever have. Enjoy it to the max!

Beauty Care for Men

Though men tend to joke that women take too long to shop for clothes and are always late for a party because they're busy beautifying themselves, most men are in fact equally self-conscious about their appearance. Well, menfolk, it's no sin to improve your looks!

Having read the e-book until this page, you must be expecting to see some recipes for homemade beauty products for men. Well, there are not going to be any—for the simple reason that men can use all the products that are made for women. You may wonder why, then, there are separate beauty products for men and women in the supermarket. The reason is quite simple. Any industry hopes to expand so it can reach a wider audience, and the beauty products industry is no exception. So they make products with different packaging, different fragrances, and different moisturizing effects. Still, men can use women's homemade natural beauty products, and women can use men's. But we do have a few beauty tips for men here.

Men Hair Care

Here are some tips to maintain hair health.

- Never over-wash your hair as this can lower the pH level and rob your hair of natural oils. Also, shampooing once a week is good for your hair.
- Wash your hair with eggs once a month.
- Use natural conditioner twice or thrice a week so your hair stays moisturized.
- Do not rub your hair aggressively after bathing as hair is weaker when wet. Just patting your hair dry will do.

121

- Once your hair starts thinning, change your hairstyle to keep up.
- Apply honey to your hair. Rinse off after 15 minutes.
- To repair your hair: Extract the juice from one lemon and add it to a mug of water. After washing your hair, pour the lemon-juice-infused water on your hair. Rinse with pure water after one minute.

Men Face Care

Face creams, moisturizers and lotions aren't just for women. As mentioned above, you can use all these products as needed.

- Never forget to cleanse, tone and moisturize. And apply sunscreen. Sunshine or rain, nature is not partial to men. You are exposed to the same weather conditions as women are.
- Exfoliate your face regularly. Exfoliation not only removes dirt but also softens your hair follicles so you can enjoy smooth shaving.
- If you have a beard, attend to it with the same care you show the hair on your head. Keep it clean, but also remember not to use shampoo too often.
- You don't want wrinkles under your eyes when your woman possesses a gorgeously youthful appearance! Take care of the skin under your eyes. Apply eye cream and keep the skin hydrated.

Homemade Shaving Cream

If you have been shaving for a while, you surely know which razor suits you best. However, even the best razor can sometimes leave you with cuts during shaving. Just apply honey to the affected skin to quicken healing.

If you have been hunting for the right shaving cream with little success, here is some good news for you. You can make your own shaving cream whenever you like.

Thoroughly mix some shea butter with coconut oil or olive oil, or both. Here is your shaving cream! You are sure to love how it feels.

Manicure and Pedicure

If you wonder whether manicures and pedicures are for men, well, they are. You don't have to paint your nails, but having them manicured will leave them clean, and your hands will look great after the nails are filed down and the cuticles are shaped. You don't need to visit a beauty salon to get the job done, either.

Body Hair

There are two broad options for those with excessive body hair: shave it or have it. Shaving is the cheapest method to remove excessive body hair, be it on the chest or legs. Waxing works great, but it can be pretty painful if used to remove chest hair! Still, it can be very effective if you don't mind the pain. There are other procedures available, including laser technology, but we are considering only natural options.

Men Grooming Kit

Grooming kits are not only for women. Men, for reasons best known to them, don't discuss these things with other men. But when they're traveling, men always carry some sort of a kit, even if they don't call it a grooming kit, containing all their essential personal care items. If you often find you've left something out of your kit, here's a checklist to get you going.

- Hair cream
- Hair brush
- Shaving cream
- Razor with blades
- Aftershave lotion
- Shampoo
- Conditioner
- Face wash
- Face moisturizer
- Body moisturizer
- Toothbrush
- Toothpaste
- Deodorant
- Manicure set

As mentioned, this is only to get you started. Add everything else you believe you will need and make your grooming kit a reliable travel companion!

Tips for a Healthy Lifestyle

Regardless of the homemade cosmetics you use, your appearance is only as good as your health. If you enjoy wonderful health, you are naturally beautiful. (Of course, you can still make beauty products at home and use them to enhance that beauty.) To live your life to the fullest, you should be healthy in every way possible. Here are the most important tips for a healthy lifestyle.

1) Eat a Balanced Diet

If "diet" sounds like a disagreeable word to you, you should really be reviewing your food habits. Having a planned diet goes a long way toward keeping you healthy. Just remember to follow the basics:

- Never skip your breakfast.
- Eat three meals a day.
- Ensure you get your share of protein, nutrients and minerals with every meal you have.
- Increase your intake of fresh and seasonal fruits and vegetables.
- Avoid junk foods and go for healthy snacks.
- Reduce your intake of white sugar and salt.

2) Increase Your Water Intake

The amount of water to drink every day depends on various factors, including your weight, your typical activities, and so on. It is generally recommended to drink 8 cups of water a day. The benefits of drinking water include:

- Regulates body temperature
- Aids in detoxification
- Lubricates the joints
- Promotes skin health and postpones the occurrence of wrinkles
- Supports weight management
- Improves digestion
- Boosts energy
- Boosts brainpower
- Supports kidney function
- Prevents cramps

3) Get Quality Sleep

Sleep deprivation leads to various health conditions, including poor immune function, obesity and heart conditions. Here is how getting enough sleep helps you:

- Gives your mind and body rest. Your body gets time to repair itself.
- Supports brain function
- Supports healthy metabolism
- Reduces risk of obesity
- Improves immune function
- Boosts focus
- Improves alertness
- Relieves stress

4) Exercise Regularly

The importance of exercising can never be overstressed. You can go for any type of exercise you like best, be it yoga, strength training or Pilates. Benefits of exercising regularly include:

- Promotes health
- Builds overall strength
- Aids in weight loss
- Boosts energy
- Promotes healthy function of organs

- Reduces risk of heart conditions
- Boosts brainpower
- Postpones signs of aging
- Improves sleep
- Cures addictions
- Relieves stress
- Promotes mood
- Improves quality of life

5) Meditate

Meditation can be a great way to achieve health and peace of mind. The power of meditation is immense. The top benefits of meditation include:

- Calms the mind
- Improves brain power
- Promotes emotional stability
- Boosts self-awareness
- Relieves stress
- Relieves anxiety
- Cures depression
- Promotes self-confidence
- Improves learning skills
- Boosts focus
- Cures addictions
- Helps with healing health conditions
- Maintains healthy blood pressure levels
- Promotes quality sleep
- Improves relationships with others
- Promotes acceptance

Your life can be designed by you—you can make it good, better or best. The choice is absolutely yours. By controlling the things you can, you gain the ability to control things you never would have thought were within your hands. Like everything else, you start at the basics and work your way up to lead a life that gives you the most happiness and others a valid lesson to learn from.

Also by Josephine Simon

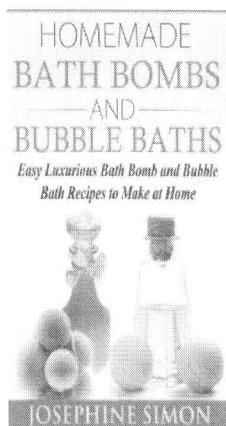

HOMEMADE BATH BOMBS AND BUBBLE BATHS
Easy Luxurious Bath Bomb and Bubble Bath Recipes to Make at Home
JOSEPHINE SIMON

Essential Oils and Aromatherapy
A Beginner's Guide to Making and Using Essential Oils at Home
FOR SKINCARE AND BEAUTY PRODUCTS
Josephine Simon

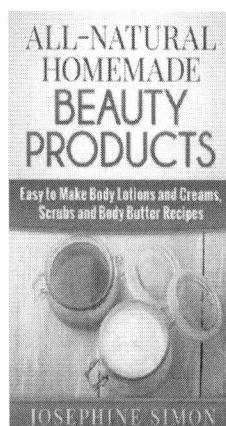

ALL-NATURAL HOMEMADE BEAUTY PRODUCTS
Easy to Make Body Lotions and Creams, Scrubs and Body Butter Recipes
JOSEPHINE SIMON

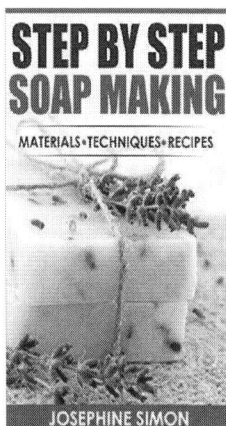

STEP BY STEP SOAP MAKING
MATERIALS • TECHNIQUES • RECIPES
JOSEPHINE SIMON

HOMEMADE ORGANIC BODY AND SKIN CARE Beauty Products
Easy to Make Lotions, Creams, Scrubs, Body Butters, Hair Products, Lip Care Recipes for Women and Men
JOSEPHINE SIMON

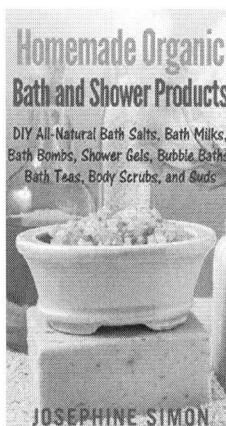

Homemade Organic Bath and Shower Products
DIY All-Natural Bath Salts, Bath Milks, Bath Bombs, Shower Gels, Bubble Baths, Bath Teas, Body Scrubs, and Suds
JOSEPHINE SIMON

HOMEMADE
ALL NATURAL MAKEUP AND BEAUTY PRODUCTS

DIY, EASY, ORGANIC MAKEUP
FACE & BODY COSMETICS RECIPES

JOSEPHINE SIMON

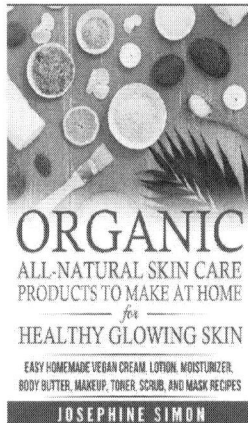

ORGANIC
ALL-NATURAL SKIN CARE
PRODUCTS TO MAKE AT HOME
for
HEALTHY GLOWING SKIN

EASY HOMEMADE VEGAN CREAM, LOTION, MOISTURIZER,
BODY BUTTER, MAKEUP, TONER, SCRUB, AND MASK RECIPES

JOSEPHINE SIMON

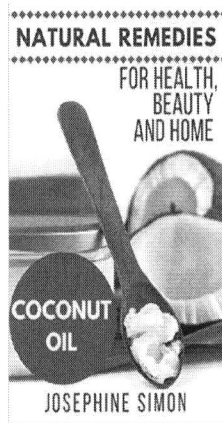

NATURAL REMEDIES
FOR HEALTH,
BEAUTY
AND HOME

COCONUT
OIL

JOSEPHINE SIMON

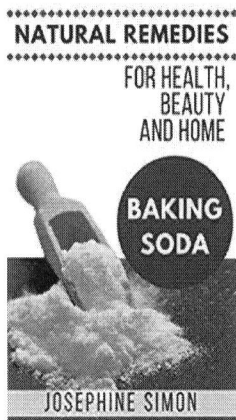

NATURAL REMEDIES
FOR HEALTH,
BEAUTY
AND HOME

BAKING
SODA

JOSEPHINE SIMON

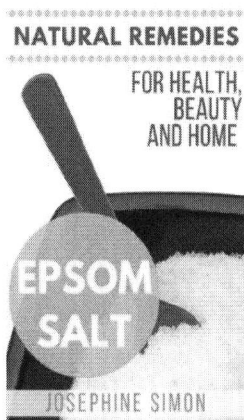

NATURAL REMEDIES
FOR HEALTH,
BEAUTY
AND HOME

EPSOM
SALT

JOSEPHINE SIMON

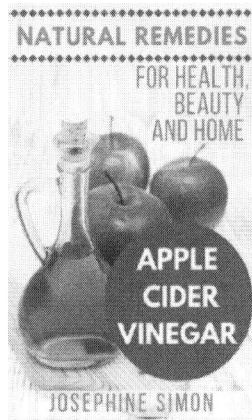

NATURAL REMEDIES
FOR HEALTH,
BEAUTY
AND HOME

APPLE
CIDER
VINEGAR

JOSEPHINE SIMON

130

Printed in Great Britain
by Amazon